CW01368100

# better together*

*This book is best read together, grownup and kid.

**a** akidsco.com

a
kids
book
about

# a kids book about social workers

by Timisha K. Wilson

**A Kids Co.**
**Editor** Emma Wolf
**Designer** Jelani Memory
**Creative Director** Rick DeLucco
**Studio Manager** Kenya Feldes
**Sales Director** Melanie Wilkins
**Head of Books** Jennifer Goldstein
**CEO and Founder** Jelani Memory

**DK**
**Delhi Technical Team** Bimlesh Tiwary Pushpak Tyagi, Rakesh Kumar
**Senior Production Editor** Jennifer Murray
**Senior Production Controller** Louise Minihane
**Senior Acquisitions Editor** Katy Flint
**Acquisitions Project Editor** Sara Forster
**Managing Art Editor** Vicky Short
**Managing Director, Licensing** Mark Searle

The author would like to thank Danielle Shelton for contributing illustrations for this book.

First American edition, 2025
Published in the United States by DK Publishing, 1745 Broadway, 20th Floor,
New York, NY 10019

First published in Great Britain in 2025 by
Dorling Kindersley Limited, 20 Vauxhall Bridge Road, London SW1V 2SA
A Penguin Random House Company

The authorised representative in the EEA is
Dorling Kindersley Verlag GmbH. Arnulfstr. 124, 80636 Munich, Germany

Copyright © 2025 Dorling Kindersley Limited
A Kids Book About, Kids Are Ready, and the colophon 'a' are trademarks of A Kids Book About, Inc.
10 9 8 7 6 5 4 3 2 1
001-349910-April/2025
All rights reserved.
No part of this publication may be reproduced, stored in or introduced into a retrieval system,
or transmitted, in any form, or by any means (electronic, mechanical, photocopying, recording,
or otherwise), without the prior written permission of the copyright owner.

A catalog record for this book is available from the Library of Congress.
A CIP catalogue record for this book is available from the British Library.
ISBN: 978-0-2417-4368-3

DK books are available at special discounts when purchased in bulk for sales
promotions, premiums, fund-raising, or education use. For details, contact:
DK Publishing Special Markets, 1745 Broadway, 20th Floor, New York, NY 10019
SpecialSales@dk.com

Printed and bound in China
**www.dk.com**
**akidsco.com**

MIX
Paper | Supporting responsible forestry
FSC™ C018179

This book was made with Forest Stewardship Council™ certified paper – one small step in DK's commitment to a sustainable future.
Learn more at www.dk.com/uk/information/sustainability

This book was written for all the supportive people I've encountered in my life—too many to name, but none who I've forgotten.

Thank you for inspiring me to become who I am today.

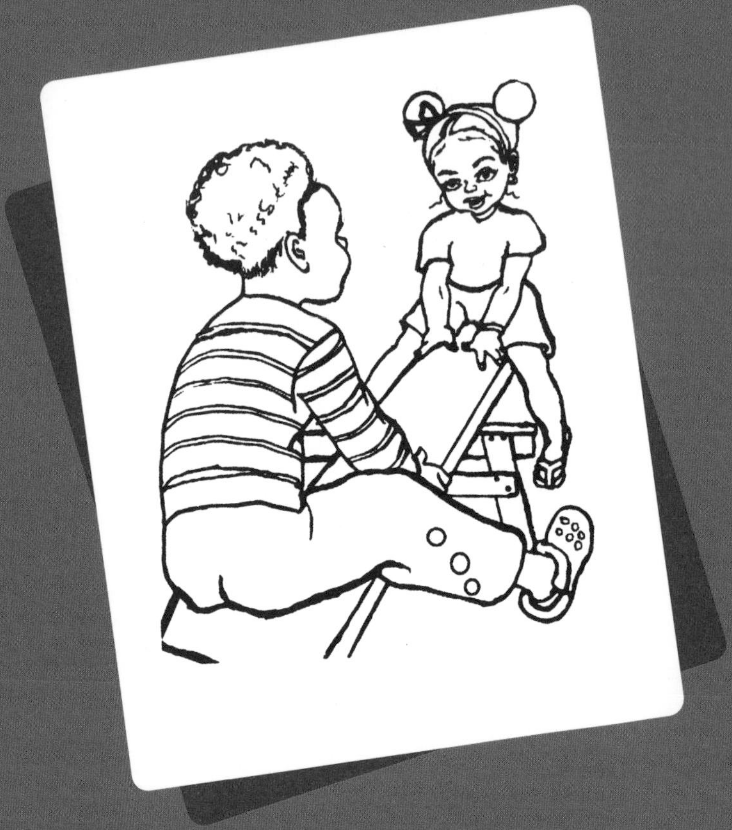

# Intro
## for grownups

Thank you for your willingness to explore more about social work! Social workers are involved in almost every situation where people work with others to get the things they need—food, safe shelter, even healthcare, to name a few. Social work means different things to different people, but overall, it's about caring people stepping in to help others who really need it.

Social workers live and work all over the world. The social work profession was created in the late 1900s to help ensure immigrants and other vulnerable populations were able to gain the tools and skills necessary in order to thrive. To this day, social workers are there to help people through the challenges they face and make sure they're equipped to do so.

For me, growing up was a fun experience, but it had its scary moments as well. I am so glad I had social workers in my life to care for me and my family and help us grow.

# Hi!
My name is Timisha.

I'm a social worker.

And if you don't know
what social work is...

I'm glad you're here!

A social worker is...

# someone loves to

who
help
others.

Social workers are all kinds
of people, of every gender,
and diverse ethnicities. They have
different abilities and ideas about
how they can help others.

They work with families and individuals to help them get to a better place in their lives.

Depending on where you live, most people have access to a social worker if they need one.

When I was a little kid, my siblings and I had social workers in our lives to help our parents access more resources and become more knowledgeable about taking care of us.

These social workers listened to us, got my parents into programs that could help them, and made sure we saw our parents regularly when my siblings and I went to live with our aunt for a little while.

When I became a grownup, I knew I wanted to do the same for other people.

I started by working with **counselors** who have a passion for helping people with disabilities find meaningful work.

(This is another kind of social work!)

I got to interact with people when they came for their appointments and I made sure the counselors had what they needed to help their clients.

During this time, I remembered how important I felt, as a kid, when someone took care of me and made sure

# my needs

# were met.

These memories created a passion inside me to care for other kids and families.

So, following my first job, I started working in **child welfare** as a **protective services caseworker**.

What does that mean?

Well, it's important that kids are safe in their homes.

We want all kids to have the things they need to thrive.

**BUT NOT ALL FAMILIES HAVE THE TOOLS TO CREATE THIS SAFE, NURTURING ENVIRONMENT.**

That's when a caseworker may need to step in—to come check on the kids.

A caseworker is alerted when there may be an issue through a report filed by someone who really cares about those kids.

Sometimes, things are OK and families just need some extra support.

Sometimes, kids may need to live somewhere else for a while.

And this can be temporary, and it can sometimes be forever.

That was job

a difficult for me!

There are so many families out there who benefit from this kind of social work.

I love when parents are able to learn how to better help their families stay together, growing together.

Just like my family, when I was young.

I kept with it and through this work, I was able to go back to school and become more educated about social work.

So I could become the best social worker I could be!

School is a part of the journey for pretty much every social worker. In some states, special classes are required to become a social worker.

Maybe that sounds like something you're already planning to do, or maybe you're thinking,

*"My goodness...even more school?!"*

And I feel you!

But I'll tell you a secret:

when you find something you really, really love, learning as much as you can about it feels pretty exciting.

No for real, I'm serious! And that's how I feel about social work.

So, where else can you find social workers?

They work in
# medical care,
# education,
# policy development*,
and even in the
# legal system.

*Policy development means creating systems
and rules to help people.

Social workers help ever

# yone

from little babies to elderly grownups.

They can teach, write books, produce movies, or be attorneys, doctors, therapists, mentors, parents—**really, anyone!**

Maybe you're wondering, how did social work start?

When the United States of America was founded, people immigrated here from several countries.

They spoke a lot of different languages and came from many backgrounds, so communicating with each other could be tough.

And often, people had a difficult time getting the resources they needed to build their lives.

But, there were people who saw these issues and wanted to help others get what they needed to thrive in their new home.

Today, social workers still help those in the United States who have been marginalized,* oppressed,** or kept from what they need to survive.

*Someone who is marginalized is made to feel unimportant or less than others.

**Someone who is oppressed has unequal burdens put on them by authority figures.

# IT'S A BIG JOB!

And it takes a lot of people for it to work the best.

To make a difference, a social worker must be trustworthy. The people who need the help of a social worker must feel they can trust in them.

People in vulnerable situations need to feel safe around others.

**Looking** like them, speaking like them, and sharing lived or cultural experiences can go a

**long way in making someone feel comfortable.**

That's why it really matters that all kinds

of people get involved in *social work*.

Do you know a social worker?

I bet you do!

Tell them, "Thank you!" for the hard work they do.

And if you've ever felt joy from helping someone else, then you may be a

Social worker at heart!

# Outro
## for grownups

I've been lucky enough to experience the care of social workers throughout my life. And their involvement inspired me so much, I became one! I hope this book encourages a curiosity about social work and the power in helping others overcome obstacles.

I believe social workers are superheroes dedicated to solving people's problems and helping them cope with difficult times. I feel so grateful to be trusted in this kind of work and I carry the influence of those early social workers with me wherever I go.

Want to learn even more? I'm so glad! There are several famous social workers you can check out: Jane Addams, Frances Perkins, Harry Hopkins, Ida B. Wells, Ruby Pernell, Whitney M. Young Jr., and Dorothy Height. Have fun exploring!

## About The Author

Timisha (she/they) is the owner of Wilson Family Services, a mental health practice in Portland, Oregon, providing therapeutic options as well as consultation and facilitation services. She is the mother of 1 college-aged grownup and is a native Oregonian. She spends most of her free time with family and friends, and just being in her community!

Timisha received her Bachelor of Science in business administration from the University of Oregon in 2003, and her Master of Social Work from Portland State University in 2012. She has worked for the Department of Human Services in Child Welfare for over a decade, and also for Portland Public Schools as a qualified mental health provider and school social worker.

Timisha remains committed to supporting the local arts, collaborating with community providers, and grounding herself by traveling and engaging in routine self-care activities.

@socialworkermish     @timishawilson

# Made to empower.

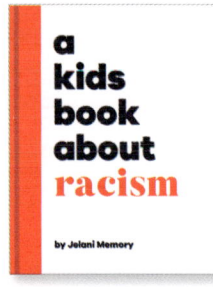

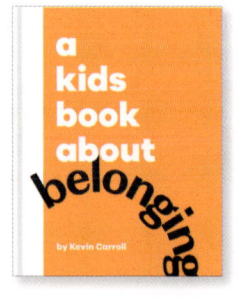

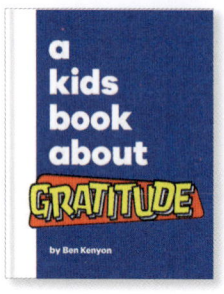

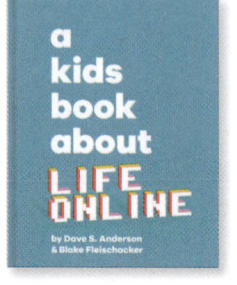

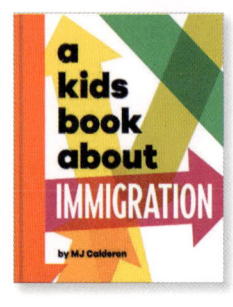

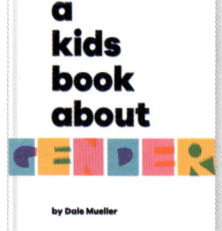

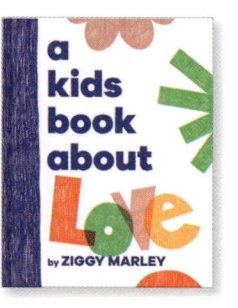

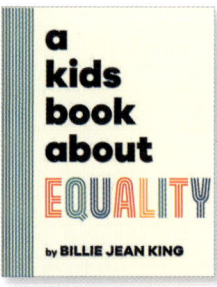

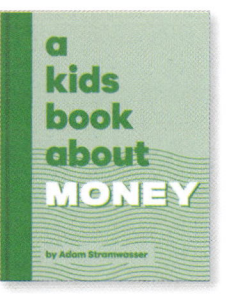

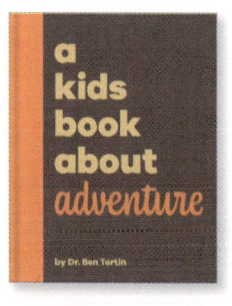

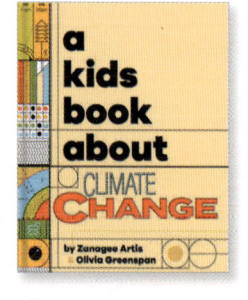

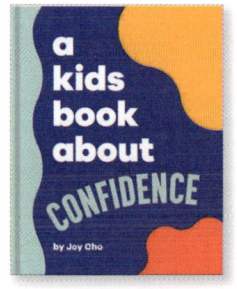

Discover more at akidsco.com